The AD/HD Forms Book

The AD/HD Forms Book

Identification, Measurement, and Intervention

Michael J. Asher • Steven B. Gordon

Research Press ▪ 2612 North Mattis Avenue ▪ Champaign, Illinois 61822

Composition by Suzanne Wagner
Cover design by Linda Brown, Positive I.D. Graphic Design, Inc.
Printed by McNaughton & Gunn, Inc.

ISBN 0–87822–378–9

Contents

Preface . . . . *vii*

Acknowledgments . . . . *ix*

Part 1: Problem Identification

Problem Identification Questionnaire 2

AD/HD Rating Scale 6

Pinpointing Form 10

Part 2: Measurement and Functional Analysis

Behavior Scorecard 14

Scatter Plot 16

Functional Analysis Questionnaire 18

Interval Recording/Time Sampling Scorecard 24

Part 3: Interventions

Coaching for Change Forms 28

Relationship Enhancement Procedure 29

Rule Establishment Procedure 30

Rule Review Procedure 32

Rule Compliance Procedure 34

Rule Violation Procedure: Primary Grades 36

Rule Violation Procedure: Secondary Grades 38

Rule Violation Procedure: Home Use (Children to Age 12) 40

Rule Violation Procedure: Home Use (Children over Age 12) 42

Plan Ahead Procedure 44

Social Buddy Procedure 45

Frequent Feedback Procedure 47

Educational Accommodation Plan 50

School Environment Learning Program (SELP) 58

Home Environment Learning Program (HELP) 72

How to Solve a Problem (HOTSAP) 84

3-D Approach 88

Social Skills Contract 92

Social Stories 96

Stop and Think Planning Essay 98

Behavior Contract and Behavior Contract Scorecards 100

Cue and Review 104

Behavior Modification Intervention Checklist 110

Reinforcement Inventories for Children and Adolescents 112

About the Authors *117*

Preface

Helping a child or adolescent with Attention-Deficit/Hyperactivity Disorder (AD/HD) is a little like planting a row of trees. The difficulty is not in knowing what to do, but rather in doing what you know. Although many texts about AD/HD exist, teachers, parents, and mental health professionals are often left with the task of taking general concepts and figuring out how to apply them. The purpose of this book is to facilitate the use of well-established strategies and procedures for working with children and adolescents who have AD/HD—in other words, to help translate knowledge into action.

The forms collected here are grouped into three parts: Problem Identification, Measurement and Functional Analysis, and Interventions. Each item is prefaced by a brief description of purpose and use and, unless noted otherwise, may be used by parents, school staff, and mental health professionals. Our earlier text, *Meeting the ADD Challenge: A Practical Guide for Teachers,* provides a context for understanding AD/HD and describes at greater length many of the procedures outlined here.* Readers will find *Meeting the ADD Challenge* helpful, but this book is not required to use the forms collected here.

This text is not intended to be a "cookbook." Clearly, assessment and intervention strategies must be tailored to the functional needs of each individual. We hope that teachers and others who work with children and adolescents who have AD/HD will find the procedures implied by these forms illuminating and that they will adapt them as necessary.

Meeting the ADD Challenge: A Practical Guide for Teachers, by S.B. Gordon and M.J. Asher, 1994, Champaign, IL: Research Press.

Acknowledgments

We wish to acknowledge the countless numbers of parents, teachers, and children who have assisted us in the development of the forms in this book. The material here has gone through many revisions and has been field tested by many individuals. We are extremely grateful to those who have contributed. In many ways the work here is best viewed as a work in progress. To all parents, teachers, and children—now and yet to come—we sincerely hope that these forms will lighten your load.

PART 1

Problem Identification

Problem Identification Questionnaire

The first step in developing an effective intervention begins with problem identification. The Problem Identification Questionnaire can be completed during the course of an interview. The questionnaire asks for specific descriptions of problem behaviors, the circumstances that may elicit these problems, the interventions currently in effect, and the estimated baseline of these problems.

Problem Identification Questionnaire

Name:_____ Date: _____

Completed by:_____

*Your responses will be of assistance in understanding the nature
of this child's difficulties. Please be as specific as possible.*

A. List the child's problem behaviors, or behaviors that need to be decreased (note the setting in which these problem behaviors occur). For example, say "Getting out of seat without permission during independent seatwork in the morning," not "Misbehaves during class" or "Hits sister between 6:00 and 7:30 in the morning," not "Fights with sister in the morning."

1. _____

2. _____

3. _____

4. _____

5. _____

B. Indicate what circumstances, situations, or events you think may trigger each of these problem behaviors.

1. _____

2. _____

3. _____

4. _____

5. _____

C. Specifically describe what you do when the child performs each of these problem behaviors.

1. _____

2. _____

3. _____

4. _____

5. _____

D. Specifically describe what others do when the child performs each of these problem behaviors.

1. _____

2. _____

3. _____

4. _____

5. _____

E. Please estimate how often (e.g., ten times a period, five times a day, etc.) and/or how long (15 minutes, 2 days, etc.) these problem behaviors occur.

1. _____

2. _____

3. _____

4. _____

5. _____

F.   Please use the space below for any additional comments that you feel would help in understanding this child's difficulties.

_____

_____

_____

_____

_____

_____

_____

_____

_____

_____

_____

_____

_____

_____

_____

_____

_____

_____

AD/HD
Rating Scale

The AD/HD Rating Scale is designed to assess the occurrence of AD/HD symptoms as well as to help users understand the specific typology of the disorder. Eighteen items derived from the fourth edition of the *Diagnostic and Statistical Manual of Mental Disorders* are given in the form of a rating scale that permits differentiation of an inattentive type, a hyperactive-impulsive type, and a combined type of AD/HD.*
The scale can be completed to assist in the diagnostic process.

---

*Diagnostic and Statistical Manual of Mental Disorders (4th ed.), by the American Psychiatric Association, 1994, Washington, DC: Author.

AD/HD Rating Scale

Name: _____ Date: _____

Completed by: _____

Please circle the number that best describes the child's behavior over the past 6 months. As a frame of reference, compare this child to a typical child with whom you are familiar.

Inattention

	Much Less Than a Typical Child		About the Same as a Typical Child		Much More Than a Typical Child
1. Fails to give close attention to details or makes careless mistakes in his/her work.	1	2	3	4	5
2. Has difficulty sustaining his/her attention in tasks or fun activities.	1	2	3	4	5
3. Doesn't listen when spoken to directly.	1	2	3	4	5
4. Doesn't follow through on instructions and fails to finish work.	1	2	3	4	5
5. Has difficulty organizing tasks and activities.	1	2	3	4	5
6. Avoids, dislikes, or is reluctant to engage in work that requires sustained mental effort.	1	2	3	4	5
7. Loses things necessary for tasks or activities.	1	2	3	4	5
8. Is easily distracted.	1	2	3	4	5
9. Is forgetful in daily activities.	1	2	3	4	5

Total number of items circled 4 or 5: _____

Hyperactivity-Impulsivity

	Much Less Than a Typical Child		About the Same as a Typical Child		Much More Than a Typical Child
10. Fidgets with hands/feet or squirms in seat.	1	2	3	4	5
11. Leaves seat in classroom or in other situations in which seating is expected.	1	2	3	4	5
12. Is restless.	1	2	3	4	5
13. Has difficulty engaging in leisure activities or doing fun things quietly.	1	2	3	4	5
14. Seems "on the go" or "driven by a motor."	1	2	3	4	5
15. Talks excessively.	1	2	3	4	5
16. Blurts out answers before questions have been completed.	1	2	3	4	5
17. Has difficulty waiting his/her turn.	1	2	3	4	5
18. Interrupts or intrudes on others.	1	2	3	4	5

Total number of items circled 4 or 5: _____

Interpretation

The fourth edition of the *Diagnostic and Statistical Manual of Mental Disorders* (American Psychiatric Association, 1994) indicates that six or more of the nine characteristics in each cluster must be endorsed for a diagnosis of AD/HD. If six or more characteristics are identified from the Inattention cluster, then a diagnosis of AD/HD, Predominantly Inattentive Type, is possible. If six or more characteristics are found for the Hyperactivity-Impulsivity cluster, then a diagnosis of AD/HD, Predominantly Hyperactive-Impulsive Type, is possible. If six or more characteristics from both clusters occur, then a diagnosis of AD/HD, Combined Type, is possible.

Pinpointing Form

Pinpointing means identifying specific behaviors that need to be changed. Behaviors can be negative behaviors that need to be decreased (e.g., getting out of seat, interrupting while parent is on the telephone) or positive behaviors that need to be increased (e.g., raising hand, waiting to ask a question). The Pinpointing Form provides assistance in problem identification by focusing on observable behaviors or actions. Typically, efforts to intervene focus on decreasing negative behaviors and first involve the use of punishment procedures. This form also permits identification of adaptive behaviors, thus helping direct attention toward more positive interventions as a starting point.

Pinpointing Form

Name: _____ Date: _____

Completed by: _____

Please identify negative behaviors (behaviors to decrease)
and positive behaviors (behaviors to increase) below.

Behaviors to Decrease

1. _____

_____

_____

2. _____

_____

_____

3. _____

_____

_____

4. _____

_____

_____

5. _____

_____

_____

Behaviors to Increase

1. _____

_____

_____

2. _____

_____

_____

3. _____

_____

_____

4. _____

_____

_____

5. _____

_____

_____

PART 2

Measurement & Functional Analysis

Behavior Scorecard

The Behavior Scorecard is a useful preintervention measure of the extent and nature of a given youngster's problems. If used during and after intervention, it also provides feedback about the efficacy of any change strategies. When used to record frequency and duration, the scorecard is easily applied to discrete behaviors; when used to record intensity, the scorecard can also help measure more dimensional problem behaviors (e.g., anger). Finally, by addressing potential antecedents (i.e., cues or triggers that may elicit the behavior) and consequences (i.e., circumstances that may strengthen or maintain the behavior), the scorecard helps users develop interventions on the basis of a better understanding of the purpose of the behavior in question.

Behavior Scorecard

Name: _____ Week of: _____

Completed by: _____

Target behavior: _____

Definition: _____

Time of data collection: _____

	Frequency (number of occurrences)	Duration (number of minutes)	Intensity (1 = weak 10 = strong)	Antecedents (events before)	Consequences (events after)
Monday					
Tuesday					
Wednesday					
Thursday					
Friday					
Saturday					
Sunday					

Scatter Plot

Designed for baseline and intervention assessment,
the Scatter Plot permits brief recordings of problem
behaviors over the course of the day and establishes
the frequency of a specific target behavior. This form
allows the respondent to record time of observation,
frequency of the behavior observed, and total number
of occurrences. It is strongly recommended that this
form be completed as a pre- and post-intervention
measure so that the data may assist in assessing
effectiveness.

Scatter Plot

Name: _____ Date: _____

Target behavior: _____

Completed by: _____

In the column marked **period** *note the specific activity (e.g., circle time, language arts, recess, homework, dinner, etc.). In the column marked* **time** *note the length of the observed interval (e.g., 9:00–9:15, 9:16–9:30, 9:31–9:45, 9:46–10:00). In the column marked* **frequency** *place a tally mark each time the target behavior occurs. In the column marked* **total** *sum the number of tally marks (e.g., 4). Total these sums to obtain a* **grand total.**

Interval	Period	Time	Frequency	Total
1				
2				
3				
4				
5				
6				
7				
8				
9				
10				
11				
12				
13				
14				
15				
16				
17				
18				
19				
20				
21				
22				
23				
24				

Grand Total _____

Functional Analysis Questionnaire

The Functional Analysis Questionnaire is designed to identify the specific function of the problem behaviors children and adolescents may exhibit. By examining particular settings and the behavioral disruptions that emerge, the respondent may determine whether the behaviors are motivated by the desire for attention, tangible reward, escape, or sensory stimulation.

The **attention** variable assesses social attention, viewing the target behavior as a means of drawing attention to oneself (e.g., the class clown). The **tangible reward** variable assesses tangible consequences of behaviors that are used to obtain a desired object (e.g., tantruming when denied a desired object). The **escape** variable assesses escaping or avoiding an unpleasant situation or task (e.g., avoiding or prolonging class work or homework). The **sensory stimulation** variable assesses the sensory needs of the individual (e.g., increased physical movement during paper-and-pencil tasks or increased stimulation when a task is uninteresting). A behavior may have more than one function or motivation. Therefore, it is possible to check more than one category.

This knowledge is essential for both targeting interventions and identifying appropriate reinforcement; without this information interventions may fail and reinforcement of undesirable behavior may occur.

Functional Analysis Questionnaire

Name:_____ Date: _____

Completed by:_____

Please circle each category of concern for which you desire a functional analysis. For each behavior identified place an X under **attention**, **tangible reward**, **escape**, *and/or* **sensory stimulation** *to indicate your best guess as to the motivation for the behavior in question.*

Motivation

	Attention	Tangible Reward	Escape	Sensory Stimulation

Setting 1: Arrival at School

BEHAVIORS

	Attention	Tangible Reward	Escape	Sensory Stimulation
1. Does not follow directions.	☐	☐	☐	☐
2. Is unprepared with all materials	☐	☐	☐	☐
3. Fails to wait turn.	☐	☐	☐	☐
4. Intrudes on others.	☐	☐	☐	☐
5. Loses/forgets material for activities.	☐	☐	☐	☐
6. Other: _____	☐	☐	☐	☐

Setting 2: Teacher Giving Group Instruction

BEHAVIORS

	Attention	Tangible Reward	Escape	Sensory Stimulation
1. Looks around the room during instructions.	☐	☐	☐	☐
2. Does not follow directions.	☐	☐	☐	☐
3. Fidgets with hands/feet.	☐	☐	☐	☐
4. Leaves seat when sitting is expected.	☐	☐	☐	☐

	Motivation			
	Attention	**Tangible Reward**	**Escape**	**Sensory Stimulation**
5. Calls out without being recognized.	☐	☐	☐	☐
6. Fails to wait for turn.	☐	☐	☐	☐
7. Intrudes on others.	☐	☐	☐	☐
8. Other: _____	☐	☐	☐	☐

Setting 3: Independent Seatwork

BEHAVIORS

1. Makes careless mistakes in schoolwork/homework.	☐	☐	☐	☐
2. Looks around room during instructions.	☐	☐	☐	☐
3. Does not follow directions.	☐	☐	☐	☐
4. Fails to complete uninteresting tasks.	☐	☐	☐	☐
5. Does not have all materials ready.	☐	☐	☐	☐
6. Fidgets with hands/feet.	☐	☐	☐	☐
7. Leaves seat when sitting is expected.	☐	☐	☐	☐
8. Rushes through schoolwork/homework.	☐	☐	☐	☐
9. Calls out without being recognized.	☐	☐	☐	☐
10. Intrudes on others.	☐	☐	☐	☐
11. Loses/forgets materials for activities.	☐	☐	☐	☐
12. Other: _____	☐	☐	☐	☐

	Motivation			
	Attention	Tangible Reward	Escape	Sensory Stimulation

Setting 4: Cooperative Learning Tasks with Peers

BEHAVIORS

	Attention	Tangible Reward	Escape	Sensory Stimulation
1. Makes careless mistakes in schoolwork/homework.	☐	☐	☐	☐
2. Looks around room during instructions.	☐	☐	☐	☐
3. Does not follow directions.	☐	☐	☐	☐
4. Fails to complete uninteresting tasks.	☐	☐	☐	☐
5. Does not have all materials ready.	☐	☐	☐	☐
6. Fidgets with hands/feet.	☐	☐	☐	☐
7. Leaves seat when sitting is expected.	☐	☐	☐	☐
8. Rushes through schoolwork/homework.	☐	☐	☐	☐
9. Calls out without being recognized.	☐	☐	☐	☐
10. Fails to wait for turn.	☐	☐	☐	☐
11. Intrudes on others.	☐	☐	☐	☐
12. Loses/forgets materials for activities.	☐	☐	☐	☐
13. Other: _____	☐	☐	☐	☐

Setting 5: Leaving Class

BEHAVIORS

	Attention	Tangible Reward	Escape	Sensory Stimulation
1. Looks around room during instructions.	☐	☐	☐	☐
2. Does not follow directions.	☐	☐	☐	☐
3. Does not have materials ready.	☐	☐	☐	☐
4. Fidgets with hands/feet.	☐	☐	☐	☐

	Motivation			
	Attention	**Tangible Reward**	**Escape**	**Sensory Stimulation**
5. Leaves seat when sitting is expected.	☐	☐	☐	☐
6. Calls out without being recognized.	☐	☐	☐	☐
7. Fails to wait for turn.	☐	☐	☐	☐
8. Intrudes on others.	☐	☐	☐	☐
9. Loses/forgets materials for activities.	☐	☐	☐	☐
10. Other: _____	☐	☐	☐	☐

Setting 6: Free Time

BEHAVIORS

	Attention	Tangible Reward	Escape	Sensory Stimulation
1. Does not follow directions.	☐	☐	☐	☐
2. Fidgets with hands/feet.	☐	☐	☐	☐
3. Leaves seat when sitting is expected.	☐	☐	☐	☐
4. Calls out without being recognized.	☐	☐	☐	☐
5. Fails to wait for turn.	☐	☐	☐	☐
6. Intrudes on others.	☐	☐	☐	☐
7. Loses/forgets materials for activities.	☐	☐	☐	☐
8. Other: _____	☐	☐	☐	☐

	Motivation			
	Attention	**Tangible Reward**	**Escape**	**Sensory Stimulation**

Setting 7 (Other): _____

BEHAVIORS

Behavior				
1. Makes careless mistakes in schoolwork/homework.	☐	☐	☐	☐
2. Looks around room during instructions.	☐	☐	☐	☐
3. Does not follow directions.	☐	☐	☐	☐
4. Fails to complete uninteresting tasks.	☐	☐	☐	☐
5. Does not have all materials ready.	☐	☐	☐	☐
6. Fidgets with hands/feet.	☐	☐	☐	☐
7. Leaves seat when sitting is expected.	☐	☐	☐	☐
8. Rushes through schoolwork/homework.	☐	☐	☐	☐
9. Calls out without being recognized.	☐	☐	☐	☐
10. Fails to wait for turn.	☐	☐	☐	☐
11. Intrudes on others.	☐	☐	☐	☐
12. Loses/forgets materials for activities.	☐	☐	☐	☐
13. Other: _____	☐	☐	☐	☐

Interval Recording/Time Sampling Scorecard

The Interval Recording/Time Sampling Scorecard is used for problems that occur with a very high frequency (e.g., off-task behavior) or that are continuous (e.g., playing appropriately with peers). The scorecard clearly shows how much of the time a child or adolescent is engaging in a specific target behavior.

In using this form, the observer must first decide whether to employ interval recording or time sampling. Interval recording and time sampling are similar in that a block of time is chosen (e.g., 30 minutes), then this block is divided into equal smaller intervals (e.g., 1 minute).

For *interval recording,* the observer records whether or not the target behavior in question occurs at all during the smaller unit of time. Before recording begins, the decision will need to be made whether occurrence will be tallied only if the target behavior occurs for the whole interval or if the target behavior occurs for any portion of this interval, no matter how brief.

With regard to *time sampling,* the observer simply notes whether or not the target behavior occurs at the end of the smaller interval. For example, if a 30-minute block of time is chosen, then divided into 30 equal 1-minute intervals, the observer would note whether or not the target behavior in question occurs at the end of each minute.

Once final data have been collected through either interval recording or time sampling, the observer can calculate a percentage score by using the following formula: *number of intervals in which the target behavior was observed ÷ total number of intervals observed × 100.*

For example, suppose a teacher is interested in determining a student's responsiveness to stimulant medication. To do so the teacher uses a time sampling scorecard to show how much of the time the student is paying attention during independent seatwork. First, the teacher operationally defines "paying attention," the target behavior, as being silent and keeping eyes on the work. Then the teacher notes at the end of each minute of a 30-minute interval whether or not the child is engaged in that target behavior. At the conclusion of the observation, the teacher counts the tally marks and finds that the student paid attention on 20 of the 30 possible intervals. In this case, the student paid attention during the observation period a total of 67% of the time *(20 ÷ 30 × 100).*

Interval Recording/Time Sampling Scorecard

Name: _____ Week of: _____

Completed by: _____

Target behavior: _____

	Target Behavior	**Percentage**
Monday	⬜⬜⬜⬜⬜⬜⬜⬜⬜⬜⬜⬜⬜⬜⬜⬜⬜⬜⬜⬜⬜⬜⬜⬜⬜	_____
Tuesday	⬜⬜⬜⬜⬜⬜⬜⬜⬜⬜⬜⬜⬜⬜⬜⬜⬜⬜⬜⬜⬜⬜⬜⬜⬜	_____
Wednesday	⬜⬜⬜⬜⬜⬜⬜⬜⬜⬜⬜⬜⬜⬜⬜⬜⬜⬜⬜⬜⬜⬜⬜⬜⬜	_____
Thursday	⬜⬜⬜⬜⬜⬜⬜⬜⬜⬜⬜⬜⬜⬜⬜⬜⬜⬜⬜⬜⬜⬜⬜⬜⬜	_____
Friday	⬜⬜⬜⬜⬜⬜⬜⬜⬜⬜⬜⬜⬜⬜⬜⬜⬜⬜⬜⬜⬜⬜⬜⬜⬜	_____
Saturday	⬜⬜⬜⬜⬜⬜⬜⬜⬜⬜⬜⬜⬜⬜⬜⬜⬜⬜⬜⬜⬜⬜⬜⬜⬜	_____
Sunday	⬜⬜⬜⬜⬜⬜⬜⬜⬜⬜⬜⬜⬜⬜⬜⬜⬜⬜⬜⬜⬜⬜⬜⬜⬜	_____

PART 3

Interventions

Coaching for Change Forms

Coaching is an essential part of programming for a child or adolescent with AD/HD. The forms in this section are designed to help teachers, parents, mental health professionals, and others (e.g., coaches, bus drivers, aides, camp counselors, etc.) who work with these youngsters on an ongoing basis. Developed to help with relationships, rules, consequences, and particular problem situations, the forms specify rationales and procedures for implementation. Several involve the respondent's monitoring the youngster's behavior over time to ensure maximum effectiveness. Specifically, the Coaching for Change Forms guide the use of the following procedures:

Relationship Enhancement Procedure

Rule Establishment Procedure

Rule Review Procedure

Rule Compliance Procedure

Rule Violation Procedure: Primary Grades

Rule Violation Procedure: Secondary Grades

Rule Violation Procedure: Home Use (Children to Age 12)

Rule Violation Procedure: Home Use (Children over Age 12)

Plan Ahead Procedure

Social Buddy Procedure

Frequent Feedback Procedure

Relationship Enhancement Procedure

Name:_____ Date: _____

Completed by:_____

Rationale

It is useful to develop a special relationship between a supervising adult and a child with AD/HD. This procedure helps establish that you are there to assist or help in any way possible.

Prompts

1. Talk to the child about his/her interests (e.g., basketball, piano, Nintendo, etc.) at a time free from crisis. Listen carefully and nonjudgmentally. List at least three of the child's interests below.

    Interest 1: _____

    Interest 2: _____

    Interest 3: _____

2. Find out two areas of interest that you have in common with the child and list below.

    Interest 1: _____

    Interest 2: _____

3. What does this child know about you? Give him/her time to ask you questions. Below, describe what you told about yourself.

    _____

    _____

4. Identify a time and place to talk regularly with the child about the child's interests and the interests you have in common.

    Time:_____ Place: _____

Rule Establishment Procedure

Name:_____ Date: _____

Rationale

It has been suggested that the ability to follow rules (i.e., rule-governed behavior) is a core deficit among individuals with AD/HD. The Rule Establishment Procedure is designed to help children and adolescents with AD/HD follow rules in high-risk situations. Two to four rules for each high-risk situation are developed; these rules are then discussed with the youngster before the situation occurs. Any number of individuals may be involved in following up the procedure: parents, teachers and school support staff, mental health professionals—even the youngster's peers.

It is important for the rules to be specific, observable, positive, and anchored to a discrete situation (e.g., playground, independent seatwork, arrival home from school, homework). Framing the rules in a positive way is especially important—for instance, Rule 1 in Example 1 is a positive way of saying "Do not hit."

Situation: _Standing in Line_____

Rule 1: _Keep hands and feet by your side._____

Rule 2: _Stand quietly._____

Rule 3: _Wait for the teacher to give the signal to go._____

Example 1

Situation: _Going to the Grocery Store_

Rule 1: _Walk when in the store._

Rule 2: _Stay close to parent._

Rule 3: _Keep hands and feet by your side._

Rule 4: _Ask parent permission before touching a store item._

Example 2

Prompt

Identify specific high-risk situations. Develop rules for these situations, then write each situation and its related rules on 3 × 5–inch cards. Make and laminate several copies. Before a high-risk situation, give the target child the card and discuss the rules.

Rule Review Procedure

Rationale

Reviewing rules before high-risk situations helps the child or adolescent with AD/HD remember to use them. The Rule Review Procedure involves having the youngster commit certain rules to memory, then asking him or her to name and describe these rules before the activity associated with the rules begins. The youngster may memorize several rules pertaining to a single event, as in the Rule Establishment Procedure, or just one rule—for example, "Use an inside voice when riding in the car."

Prompt

Each time you use the Rule Review Procedure, place a check mark in the appropriate box on the following monitoring form.

Rule Review Procedure

Name: _____ Week of: _____

Completed by: _____

	High-Risk Situation 1	**High-Risk Situation 2**
	_____	_____
	(fill in)	(fill in)
Monday	☐ ☐ ☐ ☐ ☐	☐ ☐ ☐ ☐ ☐
Tuesday	☐ ☐ ☐ ☐ ☐	☐ ☐ ☐ ☐ ☐
Wednesday	☐ ☐ ☐ ☐ ☐	☐ ☐ ☐ ☐ ☐
Thursday	☐ ☐ ☐ ☐ ☐	☐ ☐ ☐ ☐ ☐
Friday	☐ ☐ ☐ ☐ ☐	☐ ☐ ☐ ☐ ☐
Saturday	☐ ☐ ☐ ☐ ☐	☐ ☐ ☐ ☐ ☐
Sunday	☐ ☐ ☐ ☐ ☐	☐ ☐ ☐ ☐ ☐

Rule Compliance Procedure

Rationale

The Rule Compliance Procedure establishes the use of positive consequences for adhering to rules. These positive consequences can be in the form of praise (e.g., "You really spoke nicely to the other children during the kickball game") or tangible incentives (e.g., 10 minutes of free time on the computer).

Prompt

Before using this procedure, identify meaningful reinforcers for the individual by completing the Reinforcement Inventory for Children or the Reinforcement Inventory for Adolescents, beginning on page 112 of this book.

Each time you use the Rule Compliance Procedure, place a check mark in the appropriate box on the following monitoring form.

Rule Compliance Procedure

Name: _____ Week of: _____

Completed by: _____

Rule 1						**Rule 2**				
_____						_____				
(fill in)						(fill in)				
Monday	☐	☐	☐	☐	☐	☐	☐	☐	☐	☐
Tuesday	☐	☐	☐	☐	☐	☐	☐	☐	☐	☐
Wednesday	☐	☐	☐	☐	☐	☐	☐	☐	☐	☐
Thursday	☐	☐	☐	☐	☐	☐	☐	☐	☐	☐
Friday	☐	☐	☐	☐	☐	☐	☐	☐	☐	☐
Saturday	☐	☐	☐	☐	☐	☐	☐	☐	☐	☐
Sunday	☐	☐	☐	☐	☐	☐	☐	☐	☐	☐

Rule Violation Procedure: Primary Grades

Rationale

This Rule Violation Procedure, intended for school use, establishes in advance that the child will receive a Yellow Card the first time a rule violation occurs. The second time a rule violation occurs, the child receives a Red Card, is removed from the area, and is placed in "Sit and Watch." The Sit and Watch procedure involves the following steps:

Step 1: The child sits away from the activity while the adult states the rule that was violated and asks the child to repeat it. The adult informs the child of the need to sit and watch how the other children follow the rule.

Step 2: While the child watches, the adult makes a point of praising other children for rule compliance.

Step 3: At the end of 3 to 5 minutes, after the child has remained calm, the adult asks the child to state the rule and say what he or she should have done instead. The child then returns to the activity.

Step 4: When the child returns to the activity, the adult offers praise for rule compliance.

NOTE: Some children may need coaching or a brief role-play in order to respond correctly to the Sit and Watch procedure.

Prompt

Ask yourself the following questions. If you answer any questions no, address these issues before using the procedure.

1. Has a warning signal been established?

2. Has the method been adequately explained to the student?

3. Has the method been adequately explained to the class?

4. Has parent cooperation been obtained?

5. Has administrative support been obtained?

Each time you use the Rule Violation Procedure, place a check mark in the appropriate box on the following monitoring form.

Rule Violation Procedure: Primary Grades

Name: _____ Week of: _____

Completed by: _____

	Rule 1		**Rule 2**	
	_____ (fill in)		_____ (fill in)	
Monday	☐ ☐ ☐ ☐ ☐		☐ ☐ ☐ ☐ ☐	
Tuesday	☐ ☐ ☐ ☐ ☐		☐ ☐ ☐ ☐ ☐	
Wednesday	☐ ☐ ☐ ☐ ☐		☐ ☐ ☐ ☐ ☐	
Thursday	☐ ☐ ☐ ☐ ☐		☐ ☐ ☐ ☐ ☐	
Friday	☐ ☐ ☐ ☐ ☐		☐ ☐ ☐ ☐ ☐	

Rule Violation Procedure: Secondary Grades

Rationale

This Rule Violation Procedure, intended for school use, establishes in advance that the child will receive a Yellow Card the first time a rule violation occurs. The second time a rule violation occurs, the child receives a Red Card and is removed from the area. The child is isolated for 5 to 10 minutes, then given an opportunity to return after completing a Stop and Think Planning Essay (see p. 98) as well as any missed schoolwork.

Prompt

Ask yourself the following questions. If you answer any questions no, address these issues before using the procedure.

1. Has a warning signal been established?

2. Has the method been adequately explained to the student?

3. Has the method been adequately explained to the class?

4. Has parent cooperation been obtained?

5. Has administrative support been obtained?

Each time you use the Rule Violation Procedure, place a check mark in the appropriate box on the following monitoring form.

Rule Violation Procedure: Secondary Grades

Name: _____ Week of: _____

Completed by: _____

	Rule 1		**Rule 2**	
	_____		_____	
	(fill in)		(fill in)	
Monday	☐ ☐ ☐ ☐ ☐		☐ ☐ ☐ ☐ ☐	
Tuesday	☐ ☐ ☐ ☐ ☐		☐ ☐ ☐ ☐ ☐	
Wednesday	☐ ☐ ☐ ☐ ☐		☐ ☐ ☐ ☐ ☐	
Thursday	☐ ☐ ☐ ☐ ☐		☐ ☐ ☐ ☐ ☐	
Friday	☐ ☐ ☐ ☐ ☐		☐ ☐ ☐ ☐ ☐	

Rule Violation Procedure: Home Use (Children to Age 12)

Rationale

This Rule Violation Procedure, intended for home use, establishes in advance that the child will receive a Yellow Card the first time a rule violation occurs. The second time a rule violation occurs, the child receives a Red Card, is removed from the area, and is placed in "Sit and Think." The Sit and Think procedure involves the following steps:

Step 1: The child is directed to sit in a semi-secluded area (e.g., the bottom step of the front hall) while the adult states the rule that was violated. The adult informs the child of the need to sit and think about how to follow the rule.

Step 2: Sit and Think begins when the child is sitting properly and quietly. At the end of 3 to 5 minutes, after the child has remained calm, the adult approaches and asks the child to state the rule that was violated and what he or she should do instead.

Step 3: When the child returns to general household activities, the adult offers praise for rule compliance.

NOTE: Some children may need coaching or a brief role-play in order to respond correctly to the Sit and Think procedure.

Prompt

Ask yourself the following questions. If you answer any questions no, address these issues before using the procedure.

1. Has a warning signal been established?

2. Has the method been adequately explained to the child?

3. Has the method been adequately explained to other family members?

4. Have both parents agreed to implement this strategy?

Each time you use the Rule Violation Procedure, place a check mark in the appropriate box on the following monitoring form.

Rule Violation Procedure: Home Use (Children to Age 12)

Name: _____ Week of: _____

Completed by: _____

	Rule 1		**Rule 2**	
	_____		_____	
	(fill in)		(fill in)	
Monday	☐ ☐ ☐ ☐ ☐		☐ ☐ ☐ ☐ ☐	
Tuesday	☐ ☐ ☐ ☐ ☐		☐ ☐ ☐ ☐ ☐	
Wednesday	☐ ☐ ☐ ☐ ☐		☐ ☐ ☐ ☐ ☐	
Thursday	☐ ☐ ☐ ☐ ☐		☐ ☐ ☐ ☐ ☐	
Friday	☐ ☐ ☐ ☐ ☐		☐ ☐ ☐ ☐ ☐	
Saturday	☐ ☐ ☐ ☐ ☐		☐ ☐ ☐ ☐ ☐	
Sunday	☐ ☐ ☐ ☐ ☐		☐ ☐ ☐ ☐ ☐	

Rule Violation Procedure: Home Use (Children over Age 12)

Rationale

This Rule Violation Procedure, intended for home use, establishes in advance that the child will receive a Yellow Card the first time a rule violation occurs. The second time a rule violation occurs, the child receives a Red Card and a response cost procedure is imposed—in other words, the child loses a significant item (e.g., stereo, telephone, etc.) upon the occurrence of a rule violation. After 24 hours, the child is given an opportunity to have the item returned after having completed a Stop and Think Planning Essay (see p. 98).

Prompt

Ask yourself the following questions. If you answer any questions no, address these issues before using the procedure.

1. Has a warning signal been established?

2. Has the method been adequately explained to the child?

3. Has the method been adequately explained to other family members?

4. Have both parents agreed to implement this strategy?

Each time you use the Rule Violation Procedure, place a check mark in the appropriate box on the following monitoring form.

Rule Violation Procedure: Home Use (Children over Age 12)

Name: _____ Week of: _____

Completed by: _____

	Rule 1						**Rule 2**				
	_____						_____				
	(fill in)						(fill in)				
Monday	☐	☐	☐	☐	☐		☐	☐	☐	☐	☐
Tuesday	☐	☐	☐	☐	☐		☐	☐	☐	☐	☐
Wednesday	☐	☐	☐	☐	☐		☐	☐	☐	☐	☐
Thursday	☐	☐	☐	☐	☐		☐	☐	☐	☐	☐
Friday	☐	☐	☐	☐	☐		☐	☐	☐	☐	☐
Saturday	☐	☐	☐	☐	☐		☐	☐	☐	☐	☐
Sunday	☐	☐	☐	☐	☐		☐	☐	☐	☐	☐

Plan Ahead Procedure

Name:_____ Date: _____

Completed by:_____

Rationale

The Plan Ahead Procedure consists of reviewing in advance any obstacles the child or adolescent might encounter (e.g., being teased or rejected). The procedure helps the youngster develop alternative solutions if these obstacles develop.

Prompt

1. List three triggers/situations that cause problems for this child.

   a. _____

   b. _____

   c. _____

2. List three alternative solutions to overcome these obstacles.

   a. _____

   b. _____

   c. _____

3. List three ways you will help prevent recurrent problems this child experiences.

   a. _____

   b. _____

   c. _____

Social Buddy Procedure

Name:_____ Date:_____

Completed by:_____

Rationale

The Social Buddy Procedure involves identifying in advance a peer or group of peers who can provide assistance to the youngster during high-risk situations. These children can prompt and reinforce the demonstration of appropriate behavior during these times. Attention must be paid to the careful selection and training of social buddies.

Prompt

1. Which children have been identified to serve as social buddies?

    a. _____

    b. _____

    c. _____

2. What prompts or cues are the social buddies to use to initiate appropriate behavior?

    a. _____

    b. _____

    c. _____

3. What types of reinforcing comments are the social buddies to use when the child with AD/HD displays appropriate behavior?

    a. _____

    b. _____

    c. _____

4. What activities have been negotiated for participation?

a. _____

b. _____

c. _____

5. What form of training will take place to maintain the Social Buddy Procedure?

a. Daily meetings (time/place):_____

_____

b. Weekly meetings (time/place):_____

_____

Frequent Feedback Procedure

Rationale

The Frequent Feedback Procedure is based on the fact that children and adolescents with AD/HD often have different feedback needs than do other children. It may not be sufficient to wait until the end of a period or activity to inform the youngster about performance; rather, it may be more effective to give feedback more frequently (e.g., every 2 to 3 minutes). This feedback can be verbal or in the form of a predetermined nonverbal gesture (e.g., a wink or a thumbs-up sign).

The frequency of feedback should be related directly to the rate of occurrence of the target behavior, as determined by baseline data. For example, if baseline data on a child's interrupting indicate that the child interrupts once every 12 minutes, then feedback should be given more frequently than the problem behavior (e.g., once every 10 minutes). The feedback may target nonoccurrence of the problem behavior or occurrence of a behavior incompatible with the problem behavior.

Prompt

Ask yourself the following questions. If necessary, address these issues before using the procedure.

1. What appropriate behavior is desired?

2. During what period or activity will the procedure be used?

3. What is the nature of the feedback?

4. Who will be giving the feedback?

5. How often will the feedback be given?

Each time you use the Frequent Feedback Procedure, place a check mark in the appropriate box on the following monitoring form.

Frequent Feedback Procedure

Name: _____ Week of: _____

Completed by: _____

Monday	☐	☐	☐	☐	☐	☐	☐	☐	☐	☐
Tuesday	☐	☐	☐	☐	☐	☐	☐	☐	☐	☐
Wednesday	☐	☐	☐	☐	☐	☐	☐	☐	☐	☐
Thursday	☐	☐	☐	☐	☐	☐	☐	☐	☐	☐
Friday	☐	☐	☐	☐	☐	☐	☐	☐	☐	☐
Saturday	☐	☐	☐	☐	☐	☐	☐	☐	☐	☐
Sunday	☐	☐	☐	☐	☐	☐	☐	☐	☐	☐

Educational Accommodation Plan

Students with AD/HD who have "substantial limitations" in the educational setting are eligible for educational accommodations under Section 504 of the Rehabilitation Act of 1973. The Educational Accommodation Plan is designed to provide parents, teachers, school administrators, and students the opportunity to consider potential educational accommodations in physical aspects of the classroom, lesson presentation, assignments, test taking, behavior/discipline, and other areas (e.g., medication, counseling, social skills training).

Educational Accommodation Plan

Name:_____ Date:_____

Grade:_____ Age:_____ School:_____

Reason for eligibility: _____

Identified difficulties: _____

_____

Effect on student's education:_____

_____

Completed by: _____

Requested Accommodations

Please check off the accommodations that would be helpful for the identified student. This list is meant as a guide for accommodations in the regular classroom and is not intended to be exhaustive; please list other accommodations as appropriate.

Physical aspects of the classroom

☐ Stand near the student when lessons are being given.

☐ Allow the student to sit close to you if he or she needs frequent, immediate help.

☐ Allow the student to sit next to another student who can provide assistance.

☐ Allow the student to sit near the front of the room and/or near good role models.

☐ Seat the student away from problem distractions.

☐ Vary classroom arrangements, allowing the student to move between learning stations.

☐ Make specific arrangements if the student has trouble copying from the board.

☐ Post a schedule of daily lessons and activities and announce changes in routines.

☐ Post the rules or classroom expectations.

☐ Post homework assignments in the same place every day.

☐ Use a classroom aide.

☐ Other:_____

How will these accommodations be operationalized? Be specific in your descriptions so that others may understand how to implement these modifications.

_____

_____

_____

Lesson presentation

☐ Consider the skills needed to engage the lesson presented.

☐ Vary the content of lessons in amount, duration, and conceptual level.

☐ Vary the style of presentation, including audiovisual, demonstration, written, tactile, and verbal modes.

☐ Tell the student the purpose of the lesson as well as the expectations during the lesson.

☐ Obtain frequent student responses and input.

☐ Make lessons brief; break longer lessons into short segments.

☐ Divide tasks into parts; give one part at a time.

☐ Allow for someone to check the student's class work frequently.

☐ Provide outlines and organizational aids when possible.

☐ Allow frequent breaks; vary activities often.

☐ Involve the student in demonstrating lesson content.

☐ Permit audiotaping of lectures and discussions.

☐ Allow the use of adaptive equipment such as calculators and spell-checkers.

☐ Provide the student with a note taker or a copy of another student's (or the instructor's) notes.

☐ Cue the student before asking questions, allow for think time, then call on the student.

☐ Help the student learn to ask for help.

☐ Other:_____

How will these accommodations be operationalized? Be specific in your descriptions so that others may understand how to implement these modifications.

_____

_____

_____

Assignments

☐ Provide only short, clear instructions.

☐ Provide oral along with written directions for the student's later reference.

☐ Check in often with the student; have him or her repeat directions.

☐ Adjust time for completion of assignments; allow extensions if necessary.

☐ Monitor the student for follow through on lengthy assignments; help the student establish timelines.

☐ Accept work whether it is complete or not.

☐ Reduce quantity and focus on quality.

☐ Do not grade homework assignments down for spelling and sentence structure errors (unless that is the purpose of the assignment).

☐ Modify homework expectations and slowly increase expectations across the school year.

☐ Use an individualized grading system.

☐ Allow the student to use means other than writing to exhibit work (e.g., oral presentations).

☐ Set up a time for morning check-in.

☐ Set up a time for afternoon check-out.

☐ Develop an assignment sheet to be kept by the student and checked by a teacher or peer tutor.

☐ Develop an organizational checklist for work and books.

☐ Present required reading on audiotape.

☐ Provide assistance in highlighting main concepts in written material.

☐ Supply the student with examples of expected work.

☐ Accept work typed, dictated, or tape recorded (by others if needed).

☐ Provide a resource for the student to obtain help to organize other responsibilities (e.g., assign the student to last period study hall).

☐ Provide the student with an after-school tutor to help complete assigned homework.

☐ Provide the student with a second set of textbooks for home use.

☐ Allow parents to limit homework assignments if evening homework duration becomes excessive.

☐ Help the student's parents structure study time at home.

☐ Apprise the student's parents about any long-term assignments.

☐ Other:_____

How will these accommodations be operationalized? Be specific in your descriptions so that others may understand how to implement these modifications.

_____

_____

_____

Test taking

☐ Provide increased time for tests.

☐ Allow the student to retake tests when performance is poor.

☐ Allow alternative means for exhibiting mastery (e.g., take-home tests).

☐ Vary the means of class evaluation to ensure that the student has an opportunity to succeed.

☐ Give tests and quizzes orally.

☐ Modify testing format.

☐ Allow the student to take tests in alternative settings to meet specific needs.

☐ Modify district-state testing requirements.

☐ Provide the student with a sample or practice test when possible.

☐ Provide all possible test questions and have the student and teacher select specific items and number.

☐ Allow the student to contribute test questions in advance.

☐ Allow open-book or open-notes tests.

☐ Other:_____

How will these accommodations be operationalized? Be specific in your descriptions so that others may understand how to implement these modifications.

_____

_____

_____

Behavior/discipline

☐ Plan for problems; be aware of possible frustrating situations.

☐ Allow for a cooling-off period.

☐ Ignore inappropriate behavior as much as possible.

☐ Train in a "keep calm" procedure.

☐ Modify school disciplinary code to address student's behavioral issues.

☐ Ensure that a target behavior is reinforced to replace the problem behaviors being punished.

☐ Expand the disciplinary procedure to include fines, restitution, and community service.

☐ Provide the student with an ongoing coaching program to assist throughout the school day.

☐ Use a behavior management program such as the School Environment Learning Program (SELP) to monitor and reinforce behavior throughout the school day. (See pp. 58–71 in this book.)

☐ Other:_____

How will these accommodations be operationalized? Be specific in your descriptions so that others may understand how to implement these modifications.

_____

_____

_____

Other (e.g., medication, counseling, social skills training)

☐ Monitor administration of medication.

☐ Report medication effects to physician and parents.

☐ Complete frequent rating scales for medication monitoring.

☐ Set time aside to build a rapport with the student; schedule regular times to check in and talk.

☐ Avoid embarrassing situations that require the student to read aloud or respond to questions when unprepared.

☐ Develop and help the student stick to a daily routine.

☐ Frequently reinforce the student's strengths and successes.

☐ Develop a buddy system to assist in getting around school, completing homework assignments, taking notes, and participating in recreational activities such as recess.

☐ Provide the student with a social skills group.

☐ Modify length of school day.

☐ Other:_____

How will these accommodations be operationalized? Be specific in your descriptions so that others may understand how to implement these modifications.

_____

_____

_____

Persons responsible for implementing and monitoring the Educational Accommodation Plan

School district's Section 504 coordinator: _____

School's pupil assistance coordinator:_____

Counselor/social worker: _____

Classroom teacher:_____

Other: _____

Ongoing communication between home, school, and outside agencies

☐ Modify parent communication (increase frequency).

☐ Schedule periodic parent-teacher meetings.

☐ Develop plans to include the input of physicians, psychologists, or other mental health professionals.

How will these accommodations be operationalized? Be specific in your descriptions so that others may understand how to implement these modifications.

_____

_____

_____

School Environment Learning Program

The School Environment Learning Program (SELP) has proven successful in helping teachers, parents, and mental health professionals establish more positive classroom behaviors. Specifically, this program offers a means to establish a baseline and monitor four essential school behaviors: following class rules, completing class work or participating in class (whichever is appropriate), completing homework, and getting along with other students. The program makes use of school and/or home consequences to improve behavior in these four areas.

School Environment Learning Program (SELP)

Introduction

SELP is a structured program to improve school performance, designed to be implemented by the teachers and parents of children and adolescents described as lacking in self-control. These students often display behaviors that interfere not only with their own learning but with the learning of their classmates as well. Ranging from preschool age through adolescence, they are often diagnosed by mental health professionals as having AD/HD, oppositional defiant disorder, and/or conduct disorder. Within a school setting these youngsters may or may not be classified; if so, they may be considered perceptually impaired, neurologically impaired, emotionally disturbed, or perhaps socially maladjusted. The SELP program has also been used successfully with underachieving youngsters who are within the normal range of adjustment.

SELP focuses on common problem areas in the school setting and uses school and/or home consequences to improve school performance. It requires an active commitment on the part of teachers and parents, for they will be the ones actually carrying out the program, in consultation with a child study team member, principal, guidance counselor, or outside therapist.

The program may seem a bit complicated initially, but it is easily understood once put into effect. Significant success is likely in any setting willing to take the time to implement SELP. It is important to note, however, that the program needs to be conducted as written to ensure its integrity, as modifications may decrease effectiveness. By conducting the program as written, teachers, parents, and students will be able to experience the benefits of improved academic and social behaviors.

The rest of this discussion describes program procedures and the use of all necessary forms: the Behavior Rating Scale, Daily Scorecard, Reward Menu for Home/School Privileges, and Weekly Record Sheet. Samples of these forms are included in a case example illustrating program use; reproducible versions appear at the end of this section.

Summary of SELP Program Rules

1. Each school day of the week is divided into time periods. These time periods can be times of day (e.g., 9:00–9:30, 9:31–10:00, etc.), or they can correspond to specific academic periods (e.g., reading group, arithmetic, etc.).

2. After each period, the teacher uses the SELP Behavior Rating Scale to assess the student on four Target Behaviors: follows class rules, completes class work or participates in class (whichever is appropriate), completes homework, and gets along with other students.

   > Ratings of 4, 2, or 0 are entered on a Daily Scorecard.
   > If a behavior category does not apply, the period is
   > marked with an X.

3. Initial scoring is done privately for 5 days, without informing the student, in order to establish a pretreatment baseline or "behavioral X-ray." This is done to ensure that the program begins at the student's correct level of performance rather than at a level based on unrealistic expectations.

4. Teachers and/or parents establish Basic Privileges at school and/or at home. These privileges consist of approximately four activities that are significant to the child and that can be controlled (e.g., use of TV for the day, going outside, bedtime, recess, free time in class, computer time, etc.).

5. The student needs a predetermined number of points in order to obtain Basic Privileges. The number of points required is the baseline average plus 10 points.

   > For example, if after a 5-day period of private record-
   > keeping it is found that the child earns an average of
   > 20 points per day, then the number of points required
   > for Basic Privileges would be 30 points per day.

6. At the end of each school day the teacher and/or parent, with the student's assistance, enters the total number of points earned that day, then informs the student whether or not Basic Privileges have been earned. These Basic Privileges will be available during the remainder of the day at home or at school the following day.

7. At the end of each day the student has an opportunity to discuss his or her performance in a meeting to help the student improve in areas of deficiency. This meeting includes:

> Feedback about the achievement of good ratings

> Review of skills the child has employed to meet the criteria for performance (e.g., how he or she was able to obtain a 4 in the category "Gets along with other students")

> Development of strategies for progress (e.g., training the child to ask the teacher to move his or her seat)

8. All points earned must be used for Basic Privileges whether the child wants them or not. This means that the child cannot decide to forego spending points for Basic Privileges in order to deposit them into Savings and thereby use them to purchase Special Privileges.

9. If the student earns more points than needed for Basic Privileges during any given day, then these extra points are deposited into Savings and can be used to purchase Special Privileges.

10. Special Privileges are arranged in advance and posted on a Reward Menu (e.g., fishing = 50 points, sleepover = 75 points, homework pass = 40 points, extra time on the classroom computer = 20 points, extra gym time = 50 points, etc.).

11. If the student fails to earn the points needed for Basic Privileges, then the points earned that day are automatically lost. This does not apply to those points already in Savings.

12. If privileges are occurring only in school, then points in Savings can be used to purchase Special Privileges only when Basic Privileges have been earned for 2 consecutive days.

> If privileges are occurring only at home, then points in Savings can be used to purchase Special Privileges only when enough points have been earned in school to earn Basic Privileges.

> If privileges are occurring in both the school and home settings, then a combination of the above rules applies.

13. When the program is designed for both home and school use, Basic Privileges are free on weekends.

14. If the program includes both home and school, the purchase of Special Privileges on weekends is allowed only if the student has earned Basic Privileges for every day of the school week.

15. Every 2 weeks all points are totaled and a new Basic Privilege average is established. The goal is to challenge the student to improve and work toward more adaptive behavior.

Behavior Rating Scale

Follows class rules

4 = All rules followed for the entire period.

2 = Most of the rules followed for the entire period (e.g., runs to get in line).

0 = Breaks at least one major rule (e.g., pushes another person).

Completes class work or participates in class (whichever is appropriate)

4 = Completes 80% to 100% of class work/good participation.

2 = Completes 60% to 79% of class work/average participation.

0 = Completes less than 60% of class work/poor participation.

Completes homework

4 = Completes 80% to 100% of homework.

2 = Completes 60% to 79% of homework.

0 = Completes less than 60% of homework.

Gets along with other students

4 = Gets along with every student.

2 = Gets along with most students.

0 = One or more major incidents with another student.

Case Illustration

Michael, age 9, had been having severe difficulties in school for at least a year. Although Michael was on grade level academically, he was having problems following classroom rules, paying attention, completing class work, turning in his homework, and getting along with other children. Most recently, Michael had been showing evidence of "fresh talk" as well as excessive teasing of other children. His failures were considered serious enough to warrant numerous discussions between his parents, Mr. and Mrs. Jones, and his various teachers. Michael's present teacher, Ms. Smith, was very concerned because she noted that Michael seemed more "sad." She found that she often had to repeat herself over and over to get him to listen. When this would fail, she had to resort to reprimands, warnings, detentions, and parent conferences. Nothing seemed to work.

The school psychologist conducted interviews with Mr. and Mrs. Jones, Michael, and his teacher. Psychological testing and a learning evaluation were used to gather more information. A sharing conference with all parties resulted in a treatment plan that would begin with the implementation of SELP.

First, a 5-day baseline was taken without Michael's knowledge to determine his level of performance on each of the four Target Behaviors. Baseline performance was recorded on the Daily Score-card. It was found that Michael had some very good days and some very bad days, with points earned per day ranging from a high of 65 to a low of 10, with an average of 28 points per day. As a result, it was determined that Michael would need to earn 38 points per day (28 + 10) to earn his Basic Privileges.

Mr. and Mrs. Jones consulted a list of reinforcers like the ones beginning on page 112 of this book to develop Basic Privileges and Special Privileges for Michael. Once they had recorded these privileges on a Reward Menu for Home/School Privileges, they were ready to explain the program to Michael. Prepared for a less than enthusiastic response, they were surprised to learn that Michael was eager to have the opportunity to gain Special Privileges and seemed to look forward to the start of the program.

SELP began, and for the first few days Michael did quite well, earning all his Basic Privileges. However, Mr. and Mrs. Jones were wise enough to know that this was the "honeymoon period." Sure enough, Michael had a terrible day, gained no privileges, had a major temper tantrum, tore up all the recording forms, and actually ran away from home for a few hours. When he finally returned, his parents calmly told him he needed to tape the forms together and that they were going to continue to follow the program.

Every week, Michael's parents compiled the scores from the Daily Scorecard on a Weekly Record Sheet to record Michael's progress. Every 2 weeks, they averaged the number of points Michael had earned and revised the points required for him to purchase Basic Privileges by adding 10 to that average.

Over the next few months, Michael began to show steady improvement. Occasionally, setbacks would occur, but when they did they were generally less frequent, less intense, and of shorter duration. Michael was gradually weaned from the program by entering a phase of self-monitoring whereby he rated his own behavior and checked his ratings against those of his parents.

Mr. and Mrs. Jones continued to use the program independent of formal therapy for the remainder of the school year and discontinued its use over the summer when Michael was away at camp. At the start of the new school year, both parents noted significant improvements in Michael's overall behavior and did not feel a need to reinstate SELP.

Michael's Daily Scorecard

Name: _Michael_ _____ Date: _April 17_ _____

Please rate this student in each category listed below as to his/her performance during your class period/subject:

4 = Excellent
2 = Fair
0 = Poor
X = Not applicable

Class Period/Subject

Category	1	2	3	4	5	6	7	8	9	10	Total
Follows class rules	2	0	2	0	0	0	4	2	0		10
Completes class work/participates	2	2	2	0	X	2	2	4	0		14
Completes homework	X	2	2	X	X	X	2	X	X		6
Gets along with other students	0	2	0	0	0	0	2	2	2		8
Teacher's initials	NS	NS	NS	RF	RF	RF	RF	RF	NS		
Total	4	6	6	0	0	2	10	8	2		38

Comments: _Michael seemed to have a rough day today. He and I had some time_

to talk about how to turn his performace around for tomorrow, and

he seemed eager to bring up his scores.

Michael's Reward Menu for Home/School Privileges

Name: _____Michael_____ Date: ___April 18_____

Basic Privileges   Points Required

1. _Use of TV_
2. _Use of telephone_
3. _Going outside_   38
4. _Having a friend over_

Basic Privileges must be purchased every day.

Special Privileges   Points Required

1. Extended 30-minute bedtime	5
2. Snack treat	5
3. Use of bike	10
4. Extended 1-hour bedtime (weekends)	10
5. Chore pass	10
6. Choosing dinner menu	10
7. Renting a video	15
8. One friend sleeps over	15
9. Using power tools (with supervision)	25
10. Amusement park	50
11. 10-dollar gift certificate	50
12. Two friends sleep over	100

Special Privileges in school can only be purchased if all Basic Privileges
have been earned for 2 consecutive days.

Michael's Weekly Record Sheet

Name: _____Michael_____

Week beginning: _____May 6_____

Points required for Basic Privileges: _____50_____

Points carried over from previous week: _____35_____

	Points Earned	Points Spent	Savings
Monday	58	50	43
Tuesday	62	50 + 10	45
Wednesday	49	0	45
Thursday	65	50 + 25	35
Friday	30	0	35
Saturday	Basic Privileges Free		35
Sunday	Basic Privileges Free		35

Note. On Wednesday and Friday, Michael earned fewer than 50 points, the number required for Basic Priviledges. He therefore lost the points he did earn on those days.

Daily Scorecard

Name:_____ Date: _____

Please rate this student in each category listed below as to his/her performance during your class period/subject:

4 = Excellent
2 = Fair
0 = Poor
X = Not applicable

Class Period/Subject

Category	1	2	3	4	5	6	7	8	9	10	Total
Follows class rules	☐	☐	☐	☐	☐	☐	☐	☐	☐	☐	_____
Completes class work/participates	☐	☐	☐	☐	☐	☐	☐	☐	☐	☐	_____
Completes homework	☐	☐	☐	☐	☐	☐	☐	☐	☐	☐	_____
Gets along with other students	☐	☐	☐	☐	☐	☐	☐	☐	☐	☐	_____
Teacher's initials	☐	☐	☐	☐	☐	☐	☐	☐	☐	☐	
Total	☐	☐	☐	☐	☐	☐	☐	☐	☐	☐	_____

Comments: _____

_____

_____

_____

Reward Menu for Home/School Privileges

Name:_____ Date: _____

Basic Privileges   **Points Required**

1._____

2._____

3._____

4._____

_____

Basic Privileges must be purchased every day.

Special Privileges   **Points Required**

1._____   _____

2._____   _____

3._____   _____

4._____   _____

5._____   _____

6._____   _____

7._____   _____

8._____   _____

9._____   _____

10._____   _____

11._____   _____

12._____   _____

Special Privileges in school can only be purchased if all Basic Privileges
have been earned for 2 consecutive days.

Weekly Record Sheet

Name: _____

Week beginning: _____

Points required for Basic Privileges: _____

Points carried over from previous week: _____

	Points Earned	**Points Spent**	**Savings**
Monday	_____	_____	_____
Tuesday	_____	_____	_____
Wednesday	_____	_____	_____
Thursday	_____	_____	_____
Friday	_____	_____	_____
Saturday	Basic Privileges Free	_____	_____
Sunday	Basic Privileges Free	_____	_____

Home Environment Learning Program

The Home Environment Learning Program (HELP) is designed to assist parents and mental health professionals in establishing more positive home behaviors. This program provides a means to establish a baseline and monitor the behaviors required of children and adolescents at home. As is the case for the SELP, significant success is possible as a result of this program.

Home Environment Learning Program (HELP)

Introduction

HELP is a structured program designed to be implemented within the home setting by parents of children and adolescents described as lacking in self-control. These youngsters, ranging from preschool age through adolescence, are often diagnosed by mental health professionals as having AD/HD, oppositional defiant disorder, or conduct disorder. Within a school setting these youngsters may or may not be classified. When classified they may be considered perceptually impaired, neurologically impaired, emotionally disturbed, or socially maladjusted. The HELP program has also been used successfully with youngsters within the normal range of adjustment.

HELP requires an active commitment on the part of parents, for it is the parents who will actually be carrying out the program, generally in consultation with a therapist. The program may seem complicated initially, but it is easily understood once put into effect, and significant success is likely. It is important to note, however, that the program needs to be conducted as written to ensure its integrity, as modifications may decrease effectiveness. The work is well worth it in terms of improved parent-child relationships.

The rest of this discussion describes program procedures and the use of all necessary forms: the Behavior Rating Scale, Daily Scorecard, Reward Menu for Home Privileges, and Weekly Record Sheet. Samples of these forms are included in a case example illustrating program use; reproducible versions appear at the end of this section.

Summary of HELP Program Rules

1. Each day of the week is divided into three time periods: morning, afternoon, and evening.

> On school days *morning* refers to the time from waking to departure for school, *afternoon* refers to departure from school through return home and dinner, and *evening* refers to the time after dinner through bedtime.

> On weekends and holidays *morning* refers to waking through lunch (or noon), *afternoon* refers to the period after lunch through dinner, and *evening* refers to the period after dinner through bedtime.

2. The parent rates the child's behavior during each time period on a Behavior Rating Scale. The scale given here is suggested as a guideline; it may be modified to describe the behavior of the individual child more accurately.

3. The rating scale is further defined for each child by specifying observable actions that would constitute each score. For example, a score of +25 for the morning period on a school day might be defined as follows:

> Gets out of bed by 7:00 A.M.

> Dresses and washes self by 7:30 A.M. with no reminders.

> Talks pleasantly to all family members.

> Puts breakfast dishes in sink with no reminders.

> Gets to school by bus.

This type of description is developed for each time period during the day.

4. The scoring is done for 7 days privately, without informing the child, in order to establish a pretreatment baseline or "behavioral X-ray."

5. Parents establish Basic Privileges, which consist of approximately four activities that are significant to the child and that can be controlled by the parents (e.g., use of TV for the day, going outside, bedtime, special snacks, etc.).

6. The child must earn a predetermined number of points in order to obtain Basic Privileges the next day. The number of points required is the child's baseline average plus 10 points.

> For example, if after a 7-day period of private record keeping it is found that a child earns an average of 30 points per day, then the number of points required for Basic Privileges would be 40 points per day.

7. At the end of each time period, the parent records the total number of points earned and informs the child of the rating. At the end of the day, the parent informs the child whether or not Basic Privileges have been earned for the next day.

8. All points earned must be used for Basic Privileges whether the child wants them or not. This means a child cannot forego spending points for Basic Privileges in order to deposit them into Savings and thereby use them later to purchase Special Privileges.

9. If the child earns more points in a day than are needed for Basic Privileges, then the extra points are deposited into Savings and can be used to purchase Special Privileges.

10. Special Privileges are arranged in advance and posted on a Reward Menu for Home Privileges (e.g., fishing = 50 points, sleepover = 75 points, etc.).

11. If the child fails to earn the points needed for Basic Privileges, then the points earned that day are automatically lost. This does not apply to points already in Savings.

12. Points in Savings can be spent on Special Privileges only after 2 consecutive days of earning Basic Privileges.

13. Every 2 weeks, points are totaled and a new Basic Privilege average is established. The goal is to challenge the child to improve and work toward more adaptive behavior.

Behavior Rating Scale

Please make any revisions in the space provided after each rating.

+ 25 Points

Does everything that is asked with a pleasant attitude. No reminders have to be given. Gets along with all members of the family by talking pleasantly. This also applies to people outside the home. Listens attentively without interruptions. Follows instructions with a willing attitude to learn and/or take correction.

_____

_____

_____

_____

+ 15 Points

Does everything asked with a pleasant attitude but requires an occasional reminder. May have one minor disagreement with a family member, but this does not involve name calling. This also applies to people outside the family. May have one minor interruption. Follows instructions with a slightly less than willing attitude to learn and/or take correction.

_____

_____

_____

_____

+ 5 Points

Does everything asked but with some arguing. May have one minor disagreement with family members, or any disagreement involving name calling. This also applies to people outside the family. May have several interruptions. Follows instructions with slightly less than willing attitude to learn and/or take correction.

_____

_____

_____

_____

− 15 Points

Name calls, screams, makes threatening gestures or comments. Refuses to allow another person to finish speaking by yelling and/or leaving the room. Refuses to follow instructions.

_____

_____

_____

_____

− 25 Points

Punches or kicks objects, throws objects, locks self in room, attacks another person.

_____

_____

_____

_____

Case Illustration

Tanya, age 9, was referred by Mr. and Mrs. Phillips' pediatrician after lengthy discussions among her parents, teacher, and guidance counselor. Although Tanya was on grade level in school, she was having increasing difficulty following classroom rules, paying attention, and getting along with other children. Her problems were not considered serious enough to warrant a referral to the school's child study team; however, Mr. and Mrs. Phillips were very concerned because Tanya had been very difficult to manage at home for quite some time. They found that they often had to repeat themselves over and over again to get her to listen. When this would fail they had to resort to screaming, threatening, and, on occasion, spanking. Nothing seemed to work. In addition, Tanya was also beginning to show evidence of "fresh talk" as well as excessive teasing directed toward her younger sister. Mr. and Mrs. Phillips were at their wit's end, and their own relationship was starting to show the strain.

Interviews were held with Mr. and Mrs. Phillips, Tanya, and her teacher. Psychological testing and a learning evaluation were used to gather more information. A sharing conference with all parties resulted in a treatment plan that would begin with the implementation of behavioral parent training and the use of HELP.

First, the rating scale for Tanya was refined and a 7-day baseline was conducted. Baseline performance showed that Tanya had some very good days and some very bad days: Her scores each day ranged from a high of +65 points to a low of −55 points, with an average of +12 points per day. It was decided that Tanya would need +22 points per day (12 + 10) to earn all her Basic Privileges.

Mr. and Mrs. Phillips used a list of reinforcers like the ones beginning on page 112 of this book to develop Basic Privileges and Special Privileges for Tanya. Once they recorded these privileges on a Reward Menu for Home Privileges, they were ready to explain the program to Tanya. Tanya was curious about the program and seemed to look forward to the opportunity to gain Special Privileges.

HELP began, and as Tanya's Weekly Record Sheet shows, Tanya did quite well for the first week, earning all her Basic Privileges. However, Mr. and Mrs. Phillips suspected that this was the "honeymoon period." Sure enough, Tanya had a terrible day, gained no privileges, had a major temper tantrum, tore up all the recording forms, and actually ran away from home for a few hours. When she finally returned, her parents calmly told her to tape the forms together and that they were going to continue to follow the program.

Every 2 weeks, Tanya's parents totaled and averaged the points from the Weekly Record Sheet, then revised the points required for her to purchase Basic Privileges by adding 10 to that average.

Over the next few months, Tanya began to show steady improvement. Occasionally, setbacks would occur, but when they did they were generally less frequent, less intense, and of shorter duration. Tanya was gradually weaned from the program by entering a phase of self-monitoring whereby she rated her own behavior and checked her ratings against those of her parents.

Mr. and Mrs. Phillips continued to use the program independent of formal therapy for the remainder of the school year but discontinued its use over the summer. At the start of the new school year both parents noted significant improvements in Tanya's overall behavior and did not feel a need to reinstate HELP.

Tanya's Reward Menu for Home Privileges

Name: _Tanya_   Date: _January 12_

Basic Privileges	Points Required
1. _Use of TV_	
2. _Use of computer_	22
3. _Use of telephone_	
4. _Going outside to play_	

Basic Privileges must be purchased every day.

Special Privileges	Points Required
1. _Added 30 minutes of computer time_	5
2. _Extended 30-minute bedtime_	5
3. _Use of Mom's nailpolish_	12
4. _Chore pass_	12
5. _Video game rental_	15
6. _Videotape rental_	15
7. _Sleepover at friend's house_	22
8. _One friend sleeps over_	22
9. _Using kitchen to make cookies_	25
10. _Going to movies_	25
11.	
12.	

Special Privileges can only be purchased if all Basic Privileges
have been earned for 2 consecutive days.

Tanya's Weekly Record Sheet

Name: _____Tanya_____

Week beginning: _____January 26_____

Points required for Basic Privileges: _____22_____

Points carried over from previous week: ____—_____

	Points Earned	Points Spent	Savings
Monday			
Morning	+ 25		
Afternoon	+ 15		
Evening	+ 15	22	33
Tuesday			
Morning	- 25		
Afternoon	+ 15		
Evening	+ 15	—	33
Wednesday			
Morning	+ 5		
Afternoon	+ 25		
Evening	+ 15	22	56
Thursday			
Morning	+ 25		
Afternoon	+ 25		
Evening	+ 25	22 + 50	59
Friday			
Morning	- 25		
Afternoon	- 25		
Evening	- 25	—	59
Saturday			
Morning	+ 5		
Afternoon	+ 5		
Evening	+ 15	22	62
Sunday			
Morning	+ 15		
Afternoon	+ 5		
Evening	+ 25	22	85

Note. On Tuesday and Friday, Tanya earned fewer than 22 points, the number required for Basic Priviledges. She therefore lost the points she did earn on those days.

Reward Menu for Home Privileges

Name: _____ Date: _____

Basic Privileges   Points Required

1. _____

2. _____

3. _____   _____

4. _____

Basic Privileges must be purchased every day.

Special Privileges   Points Required

1. _____   _____

2. _____   _____

3. _____   _____

4. _____   _____

5. _____   _____

6. _____   _____

7. _____   _____

8. _____   _____

9. _____   _____

10. _____   _____

11. _____   _____

12. _____   _____

Special Privileges can only be purchased if all Basic Privileges
have been earned for 2 consecutive days.

Weekly Record Sheet

Name: _____

Week beginning: _____

Points required for Basic Privileges: _____

Points carried over from previous week: _____

	Points Earned	**Points Spent**	**Savings**
Monday			
Morning	_____		
Afternoon	_____		
Evening	_____	_____	_____
Tuesday			
Morning	_____		
Afternoon	_____		
Evening	_____	_____	_____
Wednesday			
Morning	_____		
Afternoon	_____		
Evening	_____	_____	_____
Thursday			
Morning	_____		
Afternoon	_____		
Evening	_____	_____	_____
Friday			
Morning	_____		
Afternoon	_____		
Evening	_____	_____	_____
Saturday			
Morning	_____		
Afternoon	_____		
Evening	_____	_____	_____
Sunday			
Morning	_____		
Afternoon	_____		
Evening	_____	_____	_____

How to Solve a Problem

In How to Solve a Problem, or HOTSAP, an adult
guides the child or adolescent in applying a 10-step
problem-solving approach. Best used when the
youngster is calm and not at the moment of crisis,
the approach requires a positive working relationship
between the two individuals who are involved. The
catchy acronym is readily incorporated into discussions with children and adolescents—for example,
"Let's use HOTSAP" or "Do you think HOTSAP
might help?"

How to Solve a Problem (HOTSAP)

Name: _____ Date: _____

Completed by:_____

Using either interview or self-directed format, fill in responses to the following questions.

1. What is your problem?_____

_____

_____

_____

_____

2. What is your goal or desired end result? _____

_____

_____

_____

_____

3. What are your current feelings (e.g., angry, scared, sad, embarrassed, etc.)?_____

_____

4. How strong are your feelings on a 1 (very weak) to 10 (very strong) scale? _____

5. List as many solutions as you can think of that have a good chance of solving the problem while reaching your stated goal.

_____

_____

_____

_____

_____

_____

_____

_____

_____

_____

_____

_____

_____

_____

_____

_____

_____

_____

6. Review each solution and decide if it is a good idea, bad idea, and why. Put a plus sign (+) next to the solution if it is a good idea. Put a minus sign (−) next to the solution if it is a bad idea.

7. Circle the solution or solutions you feel you want to put into action.

8. Describe your plan to implement your solution (e.g., when and where will you put your plan into effect)?

_____

_____

_____

_____

_____

_____

_____

_____

9. Note the end result: Did your plan accomplish what you had hoped?

_____

_____

_____

_____

_____

_____

_____

_____

10. If your plan was successful, reward yourself (e.g., by saying to yourself "good job" or "way to go"or by allowing yourself to do something special). If your plan was not successful, return to an earlier step (e.g., redefine the problem, change your goal, pick another solution, work on your plan).

3-D Approach

The 3-D Approach is a set of social skill teaching guidelines designed to help adults design and implement social skills training vignettes that the child or adolescent with AD/HD can practice on an ongoing basis. The belief is that each adult working with the youngster can identify problematic situations and then identify the steps necessary to correct the difficulties the youngster is experiencing. This procedure generally begins with a *discussion* of the specific problem impeding social success, followed by a *demonstration* of the socially appropriate behaviors necessary for success. The demonstration is broken down into practical steps that can be rehearsed by the child or adolescent. Finally, a *doing* procedure is established to ensure opportunities for the skill to be practiced and transferred to the appropriate social setting.

3-D Approach

Name:_____ Date: _____

Completed by:_____

  1. The social skill we need to DISCUSS is: _____

     a. This skill is important because:_____

     _____

     b. Identify each step of the skill.

       Step 1: _____

       Step 2: _____

       Step 3: _____

       Step 4: _____

       Step 5: _____

     c. Other people we know who are good at this skill are:

     _____

     d. Other people who are not so good are:

     _____

     e. How would your life be better if you were good at this skill?

     _____

     _____

     f. Situations that are relevant for this skill are:

     _____

     _____

2. I will DEMONSTRATE the skill.

	Yes	No
a. Show how the steps of this skill would be used. Identify the correct steps.	☐	☐
b. Demonstrate the wrong way to use the skill, purposely leaving steps out. Identify the missing steps.	☐	☐

3. DOING the skill involves an ongoing rehearsal/role-play program that should continue significantly beyond the initial discussion and demonstration. Follow the steps below and keep a record of practice.

   a. Ask the child to name the skill to be worked on.

   b. Ask the child to tell you why the skill is important.

   c. Ask the child to tell you (or read) the steps of the skill.

   d. Have the child do the steps in a role-play situation. Make sure the situation is relevant to the child's needs.

   e. Use coaching and feedback continually to fine-tune the target skill being practiced.

Use the 3-D Approach for each situation until the child has memorized the skills. Once the skills have been committed to memory, ask the child to name and describe the steps of the skill away from the problem situations (with multiple practices) and before a problematic activity or situation begins.

Each time you use the 3-D Approach, place a check mark in the appropriate box on the following monitoring form.

3-D Approach

Name:_____ Date:_____

Completed by:_____

	3-D Skill 1					**3-D Skill 2**				
	_____					_____				
	(fill in)					(fill in)				
Monday	☐	☐	☐	☐	☐	☐	☐	☐	☐	☐
Tuesday	☐	☐	☐	☐	☐	☐	☐	☐	☐	☐
Wednesday	☐	☐	☐	☐	☐	☐	☐	☐	☐	☐
Thursday	☐	☐	☐	☐	☐	☐	☐	☐	☐	☐
Friday	☐	☐	☐	☐	☐	☐	☐	☐	☐	☐
Saturday	☐	☐	☐	☐	☐	☐	☐	☐	☐	☐
Sunday	☐	☐	☐	☐	☐	☐	☐	☐	☐	☐

Social Skills Contract

Children and adolescents with AD/HD are often found deficient in a variety of social skills and may need direct instruction in these skills in order to function effectively in social situations. The Social Skills Contract is an agreement between a youngster and a supervising adult designed to encourage the youth to work on a particular social skill. It specifies the steps in the skill as well as the adult's responsibilities in helping the youngster use and master the skill. Some helpful skills and their substeps appear on the next page. A sample Social Skills Contract follows, along with a reproducible copy.

Listening and Following Directions

1. Look at Mom when she is talking.

2. Listen carefully to the directions.

3. Repeat the directions to yourself.

4. If you don't know how to begin, ask a question.

5. Check yourself to see if you are following the steps.

Being a Good Sport If Losing

1. Remain calm and continue to play.

2. Talk to others in a quiet voice.

3. Compliment whoever is winning.

4. Encourage other players.

5. Continue to be cooperative.

Giving a Compliment

1. Look for things others do that you can compliment.

2. Tell the person what you like.

3. Pat the person on the back or give a high-five.

4. Stay with the activity and keep looking for behaviors to compliment.

Going Along with Another Person's Idea

1. Listen carefully to the idea.

2. Think of what is good about the idea.

3. Praise the person for what you think is good.

4. Go along with the idea.

5. Keep your idea to yourself until you are asked to share it.

Social Skills Contract

Name: *Peter*   Date: *January 10*

I agree to work very hard at improving my social skills.
The name of the specific skill I will be practicing is:

Ignoring Billy when he calls me names.

The steps of this skill are:

1. *Leave the area or look at something else.*

2. *Repeat to myself over and over, "He's trying to get me to lose my cool."*

3. *Repeat to myself over and over, "Opinions are not facts."*

4. *Repeat to myself over and over, "I'm cool—he's the fool."*

5.

My (adult) job will be to:

1. *Meet with Peter and review in the morning, before lunch, and at the end of the day.*

2. *Provide encouragement in the form of praise.*

3.

I did my job on the dates below:

Date	Adult's Initials
1/19	*BJ*
1/20	*BJ*
1/21	*BJ*
1/22	*BJ*

Social Skills Contract

Name:_____ Date: _____

I agree to work very hard at improving my social skills.
The name of the specific skill I will be practicing is:

_____

_____

The steps of this skill are:

1. _____

2. _____

3. _____

4. _____

5. _____

My (adult) job will be to:

1. _____

2. _____

3. _____

I did my job on the dates below:

Date	**Adult's Initials**
_____	_____
_____	_____
_____	_____
_____	_____

Social Stories

Social Stories were originally developed by Carol Gray for use with those with pervasive developmental disorders such as autism.* Individuals with AD/HD may also show performance deficiencies in social situations due to failure to attend to subtle social cues. As a result, Social Stories may help to address these problems, especially for younger children. Social Stories should be written collaboratively with the adult. They involve three types of sentences: descriptive, directive, and perspective taking. *Descriptive sentences* provide basic information. *Directive sentences* direct the form behavior should take. *Perspective-taking sentences* provide information about the feelings of self and/or others. Creativity is an asset in using the Social Stories approach, as is experimentation with regard to frequency and timing of story generation. Following are two sample Social Stories, with the different types of sentences noted.

The Original Social Story Book, by Jenison Public Schools (Carol Gray, Ed.), 1993, Arlington, TX: Future Horizons, Inc.

Social Stories

Social Story 1

JON SHOWS SELF-CONTROL   *Created by: Jon and Dr. Gordon*

Jon is an 11-year-old boy who lives with his mother, father, and dog, Buddy.[1] Sometimes kids at school tease him because he takes medicine to help him pay attention and concentrate.[1] This makes Jon angry.[3] Sometimes Jon gets so angry he calls the other kids names, throws things at them, cries, or even tries to hit them.[1] When Jon does this, his teacher, his parents, and even Buddy get upset.[3] The other kids think Jon is a baby for getting so angry.[3] Jon needs to learn how to ignore the teasing.[2] He will say to himself, silently in his brain, "Stop! Calm down."[2] Then he will take a slow, deep breath.[2] Finally, he will relax his body like a rag doll.[2] When he does this he notices that the other kids have stopped teasing him.[1] If they are still teasing him Jon will do Get Calm again.[2] He will do Get Calm as long as it takes for them to stop.[2] Jon feels proud of himself.[3] His teacher, parents, and even Buddy are proud of him, too.[3]

[1] Descriptive sentence

[2] Directive sentence

[3] Perspective-taking sentence

Social Story 2

NORRINE GOES TO RECESS   *Created by: Norrine and Dr. Gordon*

Norrine is a 6-year-old girl who lives with her mother, father, and two sisters.[1] Norrine loves to go on the swings at recess.[3] She likes to go very high.[3] When Norrine goes to recess she often gets in trouble because it is hard for her to wait in line for her turn on the swings.[3] She pushes and cuts in front of the other children.[1] This makes the other children upset.[3] They tell Norrine to stop, but she doesn't listen.[1] This makes them madder, and they tell the recess aide.[1] The recess aide gets upset and makes Norrine go to time-out.[1] Norrine feels mad and sad when she has to go to time-out.[3] Norrine thinks about this when she goes to the playground.[2] She waits in line.[2] She keeps her hands and feet to herself.[2] When it is her turn, she swings as high as she can.[2] When the teacher tells Norrine to let another child have a turn, she says "OK" nicely and gets off the swings.[2] She runs to the end of the line and waits her turn.[2] Norrine feels good that she is not getting into trouble.[3]

[1] Descriptive sentence

[2] Directive sentence

[3] Perspective-taking sentence

Stop & Think Planning Essay

The Stop and Think Planning Essay helps the adult develop a point of cognitive mediation for a child or adolescent who has committed a behavioral infraction. At the conclusion of any rule violation, completing this form gives the youngster an opportunity to turn a negative situation into a learning experience. The youngster should be encouraged to respond to the guiding questions in a comprehensive manner.

Stop & Think Planning Essay

Name: _____ Week of: _____

Completed by:_____

1. What I did that got me into trouble was:

   _____

   _____

2. Three bad things that happened as a result were:

   a. _____

   b. _____

   c. _____

3. What I should have done instead was:

   _____

   _____

4. Three good things that would have happened as a result would be:

   a. _____

   b. _____

   c. _____

5. Please write a description of your plan to prevent the above problems in the future. Use the back of this form.

Behavior Contract & Behavior Contract Scorecards

The Behavior Contract is designed to address common problems that result from people's different perceptions and memories. By putting agreements between the youngster and adult in writing, these problems are greatly minimized. In addition, the Behavior Contract Scorecard may be completed by both child and adult to enable them to become more acutely aware of positive behaviors. Such awareness has the potential to improve relationships.

Behavior Contract

Name: _Brian_ _____ Date: _November 17_

Completed by: _Mr. Paradise_ _____

> *This Behavior Contract is entered into by both parties with the understanding that its goal is to produce an improvement in school and/or at home. Both parties agree to put forth their best effort.*

Brian _____ agrees to do the following:

1. _To be prepared each day for Mr. Paradise's English class_
2. _To participate and complete assigned class work_
3. _To interact appropriately with fellow classmates_
4. _To complete all assigned homework_
5. _To follow classroom rules as posted_

Signature _Brian_ _____

Mr. Paradise _____ agrees to do the following:

1. _To provide Brian with check-in and check-out assistance at the beginning and end of class_
2. _To modify assignments, allowing Brian a chance to complete assigned work_
3. _To grade Brian on participation and work completion, providing one point each day toward his final grade_
4. _To meet with Brian weekly to review progress and establish a plan for the coming week_

Signature _Mr. Paradise_ _____

Behavior Contract

Name:_____ Date: _____

Completed by: _____

This Behavior Contract is entered into by both parties with the understanding that its goal is to produce an improvement in school and/or at home. Both parties agree to put forth their best effort.

_____ agrees to do the following:

1. _____

2. _____

3. _____

4. _____

5. _____

Signature_____

_____ agrees to do the following:

1. _____

2. _____

3. _____

4. _____

5. _____

Signature_____

Behavior Contract Scorecard

Please keep score on your own behavior. If you adhered to all the terms of the contract for the day please enter a "yes" in the appropriate box. If you did not adhere to all the terms of the contract please enter a "no" in the appropriate box.

Contract for: _____

	Monday	Tuesday	Wednesday	Thursday	Friday	Saturday	Sunday
1							
2							
3							
4							
5							

Cue & Review

The Cue and Review procedure is intended to help children and adolescents with AD/HD plan for "high-risk situations" (i.e., those situations that pose difficulties on a fairly regular and predictable basis). Once these situations have been identified, a task analysis is undertaken to break the larger task down into its component parts. These parts are most commonly arranged sequentially (i.e., first you do . . . then you do . . . followed by . . .). Then a time is chosen to review these steps. The steps are always presented immediately before the high-risk situation (the "Cue") and may be reviewed as many times as desired after the situation (the "Review").

The steps are prepared in picture form for younger children (between the ages of 3 and 7) and in written form for older children (between the ages of 8 and 12). Some younger children may do well with written statements, whereas some older children may require pictures.

The Cue and Review process focuses on gradually shifting responsibility for the steps from the supervising adult (parent or teacher) to the child. This is best done through the use of questioning (e.g., "What's the first thing you do when you come into the class from recess?"). Next the adult carefully monitors the performance of each step, providing feedback and allowing the child to review his or her own performance, effectively prompting the child to learn self-monitoring and self-evaluation skills. Many would consider self-monitoring and self-evaluation skills critical components of self-control.

Virtually anything that happens can be broken down into steps and taught by using the Cue and Review procedure. Following is a sample dialogue between a father and son, illustrating the type of interaction that takes place between adult and child during the Cue and Review planning procedure. The Cue and Review Form resulting from that dialogue is included. The remainder of this section presents a number of common high-risk situations at home and at school, broken down into their component steps.

Sample Dialogue

A father and a 7-year-old son are discussing the dinner hour, a high-risk situation for the son because his older sister often interrupts him when he's telling a story about his day. The son becomes frustrated and angry, and yells at or hits his sister, resulting in his being sent away from the table. His parents estimate this occurs during 75% of the meals they have together. The son has acknowledged that this is a problem, and the father is developing a Cue and Review plan.

Father: So, what are the things you need to do at dinner so you don't get sent from the table?

Son: *(Shrugs his shoulders)* I don't know.

Father: What if you use pleasant talk?

Son: Uh-huh.

Father: What if you keep your hands to yourself?

Son: Sure.

Father: Finally, what if, when your sister interrupts you or teases you or does something annoying, you make a "T-sign" with your hands—you know, like the refs do at your basketball games when they call for time-out, except we'll know it stands for a tease by your sister? This way your mom and I will know you are upset, and we will take care of it so you won't have to lose your cool and get into trouble. How does that sound?

Son: OK, I guess.

Father: Well, let's look at those three steps. First, pleasant talk. Second, keep hands to yourself, and, third, make the T-sign when your sister teases you, and we will handle it. Here's a little form that has pictures to remind you of what you need to do at dinner. I'll go over this with you privately before we sit down, and then I'll go over it again with you privately after dinner.

Cue & Review Form

Dinner Time

1. Pleasant talk.

2. Keep hands to self.

3. Make T-sign when sister teases.

Sample

High-Risk Home Situations

Parents will need to choose from among the following situations and adapt the steps to suit their own circumstances. They will also likely need to analyze and break down other situations as the need presents: visiting someone else's house, riding in the car, bath time, going to the store/public places, playing alone, playing with other children, watching TV, having company at your house, going to a place of worship, doing household chores, having conversations with adults/others, and so forth.

Getting Up

1. Wake up.

2. Get out of bed.

3. Head for the bathroom.

Morning Wash Up

1. Brush teeth.

2. Wash face and hands.

3. Return to bedroom.

4. Get dressed.

Breakfast

1. Sit at kitchen table.

2. Eat breakfast.

3. Put dishes in sink.

Bookbag Check

1. Put homework papers in homework folder.

2. Pack lunch.

3. Pack other materials.

4. Zip backpack.

Getting Out the Door

1. Put on hat and coat.

2. Put bookbag on back.

3. Kiss good-bye.

Riding the School Bus

1. Line up at bus stop.

2. Get into the bus.

3. Sit in a seat.

4. Listen and follow bus driver's directions.

Coming Home after School

1. Walk into house.

2. Say hello to parent.

3. Remove and hang up coat.

4. Have a snack.

Getting Ready for Homework

1. Unpack bookbag.

2. Take out homework folder and put on desk.

3. Think about what homework you have to do.

4. Estimate time for each assignment.

Doing Homework

1. Read directions.

2. Sit quietly at desk.

3. Put name on paper.

4. Complete work.

5. Put homework back in folder.

6. Repack bookbag.

Free Time

1. Choose activity.

2. Play quietly.

3. Wait for directions.

Getting Ready for Dinner

1. Wash hands.

2. Sit at the table.

3. Talk with family.

4. Ask to be excused when finished eating.

5. Put dishes in sink.

Relaxing before Bedtime

1. Choose activity.

2. Sit and/or play quietly.

3. Ask for snack.

4. Clean up.

5. Wait for directions.

Getting Ready for Bed

1. Get pajamas.

2. Go to bathroom

3. Brush teeth.

4. Take bath or shower.

5. Return to bedroom.

Bedtime

1. Choose book to read.

2. Read quietly with parent.

3. Read quietly to self.

4. Turn out lights and say good night.

5. Turn on tape or radio.

6. Remain quietly in bed.

High-Risk School Situations

Teachers will need to choose from among the following situations and adapt the steps to suit their own circumstances. In addition, they will likely need to analyze and break down other times and situations as the need presents: when working in small groups, when the teacher is talking and giving directions, when lining up, when walking down school hallways, when in the bathroom, when on field trips, during special assemblies, at recess, when talking to others, and so forth.

Starting the Day

1. Hang up coat.

2. Unpack bookbag at desk.

3. Place homework folder on desk.

4. Put lunch box in closet.

5. Put bookbag in pile in front of closet.

6. Return to seat and begin work.

Independent Seatwork

1. Listen to directions.

2. Stay in seat.

3. Work quietly on assignment.

4. Raise hand and wait in seat for help.

Finishing Up in the Morning

1. Put name on all papers.

2. Pass papers in as teacher says.

Free Time

1. Keep hands and feet to yourself.

2. Play quietly.

Getting Ready for Lunch

1. Wash hands.

2. Get lunch box.

3. Sit down at desk.

4. Walk in line when called.

Lunch Time

1. Walk quietly in line.

2. Talk quietly with classmates.

3. Keep hands and feet to yourself.

Indoor Recess

1. Share toys and materials with classmates.

2. Clean up when told.

3. Sit down when told.

Completing Assignments

1. Listen to directions.

2. Repeat directions.

3. Complete the assignment.

Going to Another Class

1. Walk quietly in line.

2. Listen and follow directions.

3. Keep hands and feet to yourself.

Listening

1. Walk quietly in line.

2. Sit in front of the teacher.

3. Listen to what the teacher is saying.

Library Time

1. Sit down quietly at the table.

2. Find books when told.

3. Sign books out.

4. Sit down and read books quietly.

Going Home

1. Put papers inside homework folder.

2. Find books and other materials.

3. Get bookbag and pack it up.

4. Get coat and put it on.

5. Wait at desk for instructions.

Behavior Modification Intervention Checklist

The Behavior Modification Intervention Checklist, coauthored by Rita F. Gordon and Steven B. Gordon, offers the opportunity to review general considerations in developing and implementing program changes. Use the checklist to spot trouble areas before conducting an intervention, as well as to monitor delivery of the intervention at various times during its implementation.

Behavior Modification Intervention Checklist

	Yes	No
1. Has a target behavior been clearly defined so that two independent observers could agree?	☐	☐
2. Has a functional analysis been completed?	☐	☐
3. Has a measurement procedure been selected?	☐	☐
4. Has a period of time for data collection been chosen?	☐	☐
5. Has a person been identified to collect the data?	☐	☐
6. Does the intervention identify a positive target behavior to strengthen?	☐	☐
7. Has a reinforcement survey been completed?	☐	☐
8. Does the intervention include an attempt to increase a positive target behavior by using positive reinforcement?	☐	☐
9. Does the intervention address antecedent modification?	☐	☐
10. Are reinforcers delivered at the proper frequency?	☐	☐
11. If a punishment procedure is used, are there appropriate safeguards?	☐	☐

Reinforcement Inventories

The first step in designing an intervention involving positive consequences is to determine what consequences are actually reinforcing to the child. The Reinforcement Inventories included here list common reinforcers for children and adolescents at school and at home. These formal questionnaires can be helpful in determining which reinforcing consequences are salient. Whether used as part of a structured interview or administered independently, these inventories can help elicit valuable information about potential positive consequences for a specific youngster or group of youngsters.

Reinforcement Inventory for Children

Name:_____ Date: _____

Completed by:_____

Check off any or all reinforcers that may be effective
in this specific situation and for this particular child.

School

- ☐ Having extra or longer recess
- ☐ Erasing chalkboards
- ☐ Helping the custodian
- ☐ Telephoning parent
- ☐ Being group leader
- ☐ Going to the principal's office on errand
- ☐ Fixing bulletin board
- ☐ Using stopwatch
- ☐ Going to the library
- ☐ Tutoring another student
- ☐ Running errands
- ☐ Getting a "good note" to parent
- ☐ Being hall monitor
- ☐ Chewing gum in class
- ☐ Playing a game
- ☐ Getting positive comments on homework

- ☐ Listening to tapes or CDs
- ☐ Having picture taken
- ☐ Helping librarian
- ☐ Getting stars or stickers
- ☐ Sharpening pencils
- ☐ Being cafeteria helper
- ☐ Viewing films or videotapes
- ☐ Getting a badge to be worn all day
- ☐ Being excused from homework
- ☐ Demonstrating a hobby to class
- ☐ Having a party
- ☐ Getting a special certificate
- ☐ Getting a drink of water
- ☐ Being principal's helper
- ☐ Having choice of seat mate
- ☐ Having a snack

- ☐ Watching self on videotape
- ☐ Getting free activity time (puzzles, games)
- ☐ Playing an instrument
- ☐ Getting a happy face on paper
- ☐ Having story time
- ☐ Participating in crafts activities
- ☐ Having lunch with teacher
- ☐ Being head of the lunch line
- ☐ Making a videotape
- ☐ Other:_____

   _____

   _____

   _____

   _____

Home

Social

- [ ] Hugs
- [ ] Pats on the back
- [ ] Kisses
- [ ] High fives
- [ ] Verbal praise
- [ ] Other:_____

  _____

  _____

Privileges or Activities

- [ ] Dressing up in adult clothing
- [ ] Opening coffee can
- [ ] Taking a trip to park
- [ ] Helping make dessert
- [ ] Playing with friends
- [ ] Feeding the baby
- [ ] Reading a bedtime story
- [ ] Having later bedtime
- [ ] Playing on swing set
- [ ] Going to movies
- [ ] Spending a night with friends or grandparents

- [ ] Using stereo
- [ ] Riding next to the window in car
- [ ] Going to a ball game
- [ ] Making a home video
- [ ] Eating out
- [ ] Choosing menu for meal
- [ ] Using tools
- [ ] Going someplace alone with a parent
- [ ] Making a phone call
- [ ] Baking something
- [ ] Gardening
- [ ] Planning a day's activities
- [ ] Riding bicycle
- [ ] Choosing TV program
- [ ] Skipping chores
- [ ] Going on a fishing trip
- [ ] Camping in backyard
- [ ] Other:_____

  _____

  _____

Material

- [ ] Toys
- [ ] Snacks
- [ ] Pets
- [ ] Own bedroom
- [ ] Books
- [ ] Clothing
- [ ] Other:_____

  _____

  _____

Token

- [ ] Money
- [ ] Allowance
- [ ] Stars on chart
- [ ] Own bank account
- [ ] Other:_____

  _____

  _____

Reinforcement Inventory for Adolescents

Name:_____ Date: _____

Completed by:_____

Check off any or all reinforcers that may be effective in this specific situation and for this particular child.

School

☐ Being group leader

☐ Running errands

☐ Playing games

☐ Watching films or videotapes

☐ Playing an instrument

☐ Making a videotape

☐ Chewing gum in class

☐ Having free activity time

☐ Having an extended lunch period

☐ Participating in school trips

☐ Having the opportunity to improve grades

☐ Wearing a baseball cap in class

☐ Being in charge of class discussion

☐ Serving as hall monitor

☐ Listening to records or tapes

☐ Having a homework pass

☐ Tutoring another student

☐ Demonstrating a hobby to the class

☐ Developing a school radio show

☐ Playing a video game

☐ Being on sports team

☐ Being dismissed early from class

☐ Other: _____

_____

Home

Social

- [ ] Smiles
- [ ] Hugs
- [ ] Attention when talking
- [ ] Being asked for opinion
- [ ] Winks
- [ ] Verbal praise
- [ ] Head nods
- [ ] Thumbs-up sign
- [ ] Other:_____

_____

_____

Privileges or Activities

- [ ] Dating privileges
- [ ] Car privileges
- [ ] Getting driver's license
- [ ] Reading
- [ ] Having extended curfew
- [ ] Staying up late
- [ ] Staying overnight with friends
- [ ] Having time off from chores
- [ ] Having an opportunity to earn money

- [ ] Selecting TV program
- [ ] Using family camera
- [ ] Participating in activities with friends
- [ ] Having a part-time job
- [ ] Having friends over
- [ ] Taking dance or music lessons
- [ ] Redecorating room
- [ ] Skating
- [ ] Listening to stereo
- [ ] Having additional time on telephone
- [ ] Choosing own bedtime
- [ ] Taking trip alone on bus or plane
- [ ] Other:_____

_____

_____

Material

- [ ] Favorite meal
- [ ] Clothes
- [ ] Books
- [ ] Radio or stereo
- [ ] Bicycle

- [ ] Electric razor
- [ ] Own room
- [ ] Own TV
- [ ] Watch
- [ ] Make-up
- [ ] Tapes or CDs
- [ ] Private phone
- [ ] Jewelry
- [ ] Own telephone
- [ ] Musical instrument
- [ ] Other:_____

_____

_____

Token

- [ ] Extra money
- [ ] Own checking account
- [ ] Allowance
- [ ] Gift certificate
- [ ] Other:_____

_____

_____

About the Authors

Dr. Michael J. Asher is a licensed psychologist in private practice at Behavior Therapy Associates, P.A., in Somerset, New Jersey. He is also a consultant to numerous school districts and private schools in New Jersey and a field supervisor for the Graduate School of Applied and Professional Psychology at Rutgers University. Dr. Asher received his Ph.D. in clinical psychology from the Illinois Institute of Technology in Chicago. He conducts workshops at the local, state, national, and international levels on the topic of Attention-Deficit/Hyperactivity Disorder and other disorders in children and adolescents.

Dr. Steven B. Gordon is a licensed psychologist in private practice and Director of Behavior Therapy Associates, P.A., in Somerset, New Jersey. He has served as clinical associate professor in the Department of Psychiatry, Robert Wood Johnson Medical School, and is a Diplomate in Behavior Therapy and in Behavioral Psychology, American Board of Professional Psychology. He is also a contributing faculty member at the Graduate School of Applied and Professional Psychology, Rutgers University, where he teaches behavior therapy. Dr. Gordon received his Ph.D. in clinical psychology from West Virginia University and was a postdoctoral fellow in behavior modification at the State University of New York at Stony Brook. He has consulted with numerous school districts and private special education schools, lectures extensively, and conducts parent and teacher workshops on the topic of Attention-Deficit/Hyperactivity Disorder.